# NORMAN ROCKWELL'S
# AMERICAN SPORTSMAN

*Written by Marian Hoffman*

**CRESCENT BOOKS**
New York

Illustrations reprinted under license from
the Estate of Norman Rockwell.

Copyright © 1990 Estate of Norman Rockwell

Photographic material courtesy of
The Norman Rockwell Museum at
Stockbridge, Stockbridge, MA

Created and manufactured by arrangement with
Ottenheimer Publishers, Inc.

Copyright © 1990 Ottenheimer Publishers, Inc.
This 1990 edition is published by Ottenheimer
Publishers, Inc. for Crescent Books,
distributed by Crown Publishers, Inc.,
225 Park Avenue South, New York, New York 10003

Printed and bound in Hong Kong.

ISBN: 0-517-679000-0
h g f e d c b a

# CONTENTS

*Boys Playing Leapfrog (1919)*

# Introduction

At one time or another, sports play a role in the life of everyone. Children learn to throw and catch balls at an early age. They soon join with neighborhood friends to play spontaneous games of baseball, kickball, and stoopball, and to invent games using any kind of ball, and games that don't require any equipment other than imagination.

This interest spans generations. Children, parents, grandparents and other relatives participate in, watch and discuss sports together. Sports can enhance family life, providing a way for parents, children, siblings and relatives to join each other in an activity.

Some people enjoy sports as spectators, others as participants. Some thrive on competition with others, some prefer meeting a personal challenge. Some love sports for the camaraderie they provide, others enjoy solitary activities. For these people, an interest in sports is a way of life. Sports are a form of recreation and relaxation, a fun way to exercise and to release tensions. A love of sports can last a lifetime and can be passed from generation to generation.

Norman Rockwell characterized American sports in his earliest work and throughout his career. He caught unique moments of the jubilation of winning or the misery of losing. He portrayed these small moments with his unusual talents, and left a chronicle of sports in his incomparable manner. Stroll through this collection of stories about individual sport memories and enjoy Norman Rockwell's art.

10

*Springtime (1927)*

# Chapter 1
# Growing Up With Sports

## Memories

Childhood memories always began in the spring. Fragrant, mild breezes kindle that heady feeling of optimism, and signaled the opening of the baseball season. Something new was about to begin! On opening day, children at school grew restless, as if they could already sense the exuberance of the roaring crowd on the other side of town. A few lucky children even skipped school to go to the game, and regaled their friends with opening-day adventures when they returned the next day.

While the pros headed to the ballpark each spring, neighborhood children headed outdoors to play baseball their own way—in vacant lots, schoolyards, city streets, alleys, backyards, and pastures. If the perfect field wasn't available, they settled for what was available. Sometimes that field disappeared when the real estate developers took over a section of town.

# The Neighborhood Baseball Field

Vacant lots in the neighborhood gradually disappeared and parents in the local community organization filled the gap by finding a field for the kids to use. It sometimes was less than ideal. It usually was bumpy, weedy, and bordered by woods. Center field was a big hill. The parents built a backstop, but if anyone hit a foul ball higher than the backstop, it landed in the woods and the teams spent an hour looking for it. This was the reason the oldest baseballs available were always used. It wouldn't matter if they got lost.

Some kids grew up in the city, where no one had a yard big enough for a neighborhood ball game. So, they either played stoop ball or punchball in the street with a small rubber ball. The imagination of these kids had to work overtime. A manhole cover in the middle of the street became a pitcher's mound, and small trees growing by the pavement on either side became first and third base.

*Construction Crew (1954)*

# Baseball Fantasies

As they play, children indulge in baseball fantasies. It's the bottom of the ninth with two out and the winning run on third, and they're up at bat, hoping they won't suffer the same fate as Casey! Or perhaps they're the center fielder who just has to run and make a leaping catch to win the game. It would be marvelous to be the pitcher with a blazing fast ball that no one can hit. Everyone can be a hero for an afternoon.

Children growing up in the 'teens pretended they were Babe Ruth or Ty Cobb, playing on a team where everyone had nicknames like Slats, Cocky, Flash, Zip, or Firebrand. In the Forties, Stan Musial, Joe DiMaggio, and Ted Williams were the heroes. The man of the hour in the fifties was Mickey Mantle, and team nicknames changed to Pig, Snake, Squirrel, Weasel, and Mule. Children lucky enough to cheer on their heroes from the stands carry those memories always. Baseball provides the legends that make up childhood dreams. It affords camaraderie as well, often among children of different ages and sizes. When we are young, we are all athletes.

*The Lucky Seventh (1915)*

Some youngsters were lucky enough to grow up on a street with plenty of children, boys and girls of all ages. One family may have sacrificed every blade of grass on their front lawn for a neighborhood ball field. The neighborhood children congregated here to play baseball each summer, and football each winter. No matter how old or how big they were, everyone had a place on the team, and a special feeling of belonging.

Sharing victories, defeats, and adventures together is what creates that sense of belonging among children. The team huddles in the dugout together cheering each other on, and offering commiserating pats on the back when things don't go well. Simply sharing a glorious day with others, or being outside playing together during the magical twilight hours fosters a feeling of closeness.

Many neighborhoods had a large family, who played baseball in their back yard on summer evenings. Including the cousins who always dropped by, there were just enough family members to make up two teams. On those evenings, the neighborhood children couldn't wait to finish dinner to run over and play ball with them. The ball game went on until dusk, and when everyone heard their particular summons, they knew it was time to go home. Perhaps this was the only activity that joined this family with the neighborhood children, but on those summer evenings, everyone felt as if they were a member of that big, warm family.

Each afternoon, during the school year, all the neighborhood boys congregated in someone's back yard to play ball. At 5:30, all the mothers rang bells, blew whistles, or simply yelled for their children to come home for dinner. After a while, the children learned to recognize one another's signals, and could identify almost every mother's method of summoning her crew. To the children, all the bells and whistles blended into a single common command that every last one of them had to obey.

*Coach Quigley's Code (1917)*

Neighborhood baseball games are the domain of children. There everyone is free from parental interference. Children can make up their own rules, and set up their own systems. These games are so special because they are completely organized by kids. Grownups have nothing to do with them. Kids make up the rules and whole new versions of the game. After all, they don't have many other opportunities at that age to be so free from parental authority.

# The Pros

Not even a great neighborhood baseball game beats watching a professional ball game. What can compete with that intense assault on the senses? The sounds of the crowd swell and diminish like the surf. The vendors yell, and the smells of popcorn and hot dogs mingle with those of perfume, after shave and sweat. It's impossible not to observe the other spectators, to feel their nearness, and to be carried away by their cheers. Going to the ballpark means feeling that special surge of joy as the *Star-Spangled Banner* gives way to shouts of "Play Ball!"

The luckiest children enter the game with their own tickets clutched tightly in their hands. They push right through the turnstile and, surrounded by a mass of bumping people, walk up the dizzying path until they reach their row. Those not lucky enough to have tickets use their ingenuity to find their own ways to watch the game.

*The Dugout (1948)*

19

*The Peephole (1958)*

The most fortunate children went to a school across the street from the stadium. Sometimes after school, it was possible to find a gate guard looking the other way as a group of children approached. This was about the middle of the fourth inning, so the guards were not as concerned about the ticket requirements, and allowed the kids to enter. It was years before many of these kids finally saw the first three innings of a game.

Less daring classmates could find a knothole in the fence around the ballpark, which had a splendid view of right field. Of course, if there weren't many balls hit to right field that day, it could be a long, dull afternoon for them!

A day at the ballpark teaches children a life lesson. It is exhilarating to win, and there is immense satisfaction to be gained simply from observing the processes and rituals of playing nine innings of baseball.

Like all sports, however, baseball can bring frustration to certain children. Remember the child who gets picked last every time, the one who tightens up in a clutch and never comes through, the one who is too little or too slow to keep up with the others? Even the best and the fastest kids on the team occasionally hit into a double play, or drop a fly ball. Ballplaying teaches many important lessons of life: bouncing back after a setback, believing in yourself, making the most of your skills, and persevering.

# Playing the Game

A mediocre player found many ways to strengthen his skills. Perhaps he couldn't hit the ball very hard, but was a fast runner, so he learned to bunt. He could hit the ball so that it bounced near his feet, run like heck and make it to first base safely.

The best pitcher in school always had a fast ball that whizzed past the hapless batter before the bat could even swing. The curve ball always left the batter beating at air, feeling foolish. One day, someone finally swung at this fast ball and heard the crack of the wood against the ball. A triple off the best pitcher made that lucky hitter feel like a million bucks!

*The Indian Sign (1916)*

# Building Confidence

Each success on the baseball field gives a child a little more confidence, makes him walk a little taller. When he finally gets the winning hit or she makes that sensational fielding play, they learn, for a day, what it feels like to be a champion. Baseball can mean many different things to kids. It's a way to work off energy, and to hone skills. It teaches them about sportsmanship and about working together for a common cause.

*Keeping His Course (1918)*

# Cooling Off

Baseball season begins with the freshness of the spring, and lasts throughout the languor of summer. It fills the long, hot summer days and evenings with activity. Summer is a time when children shift their lives outdoors. In the heat of those sultry afternoons, swimming becomes everyone's favorite activity. After a vigorous game of baseball, or after household chores are done, kids head for the nearest swimming hole. Perhaps there's a secret swimming spot, tucked away in the woods, that only a few know about. The luckiest folks congregate at a nearby neighborhood swimming pool.

The appeal of swimming is two-fold. There's that delicious sensation of hot skin meeting cold water, and physical relief from the heat. The fun of games and horseplay in a different arena, the water, is hard to beat. In this new setting, baseball, volleyball, and other sports take on a whole new dimension.

On really hot days, the traditional baseball game went into the pool. The usual baseball equipment was traded for a plastic bat and ball. There was always a lot of confusion about where the bases really were-but such details didn't matter. The object of the game was just to lunge after the ball and splash around in the water.

*Girl with Picnic Basket Going Swimming* (1929)

# Water Play

Being in the water fuels the imagination. As they glide smoothly through the water, children imagine they are mermaids or sea creatures—no longer human, but amphibian. All clumsiness disappears, as the water bestows a special grace on each one of them. Water provides the illusion of being hidden from those still on land, of being protected and sheltered.

Sitting on the bottom of the swimming pool and pretending is great. It never occurs to the child that everyone can see the pretend game!

# Water Heroes

Just as with baseball, children look up to swimming heroes. As they splash across the pond in record time, they dream they are challenging Johnny Weismuller, Mark Spitz, or Janet Evans for a gold medal. They execute weird contortions as they dive into the water, pretending to be Greg Louganis. Water provides a new challenge, a new force to overcome.

# Swimming Holes

At least once a summer, the most grandiose water adventure is invented. Uncle Jim tells of stringing a rope across the old quarry and hanging a pulley on the rope. He described holding on to the pulley for dear life and riding across the rope until just over the center of the quarry. Then, let go and fall into the water! It took days to engineer and set up the device. Trees had to be climbed to attach the rope so that the pulley would start at a high point. When it was ready, nobody wanted to be the first to try it! Uncle Jim brags that it was his idea originally, so he was finally elected to go first. It worked surprisingly well, but a slight hitch occurred. Once he had jumped into the water, it was impossible to get the pulley back up to the starting point so the next person could have a turn.

*Tail End of a Dive (1915)*

29

All the children in the area went to the old quarry to swim. On one side, it was lined with high rocks that the more adventurous kids used as a diving board. There was an unspoken division among children in the quarry: the ones who had the nerve to jump off those rocks, and those who didn't. Moving from one group into the other was a classic rite of passage. Uncle Jim described the process. You climbed up the rocks, trying to work up some courage. From the top, the rocks seemed even higher and more menacing. It was too late to turn back because everyone was looking up, waiting to see what would happen. There was no face-saving way out—so you just took a deep breath and leaped. Once someone jumped off the highest rock, he'd conquered the swimming hole, and knew that anything was within his reach.

# Croquet

Any grassy area can become a croquet course. A game of croquet challenges everyone to channel their energy toward one small goal— the wicket. Croquet tests the accuracy of aim and timing.

A hilly, bumpy yard made a demanding croquet course, although it was completely unsuitable for one! The wickets were sunk into the ground. Getting the croquet ball through the wicket involved more luck than skill, because it was impossible to control the ball's path downhill and over all the bumps. The obstacles made the course exciting and challenging.

Grandma and Grandpop met at a croquet game, forever immortalized in a picture on their wall.

*Croquet (1931)*

DRAWN BY NORMAN P. ROCKWELL.

*What Sports Do for You (1914)*

# Autumn Sports

In autumn, as the baseball season finally fades away, the burst of cooler air seems to bring about a fresh burst of energy. Children begin to crave a rougher, more physical game than baseball. Football becomes the new sport of choice. Often, the same children who formed the baseball teams in the spring and summer regroup to form football teams throughout the fall and winter. Around October, baseball is abandoned and football begins. Layers of clothes are piled on for padding and warmth and safety. Also, it didn't hurt too much to be tackled. What was best about football was that everyone was part of the action. In baseball, the child spent a lot of time waiting for a turn at bat. What child can resist throwing his body around and smashing into his friends!

Collisions are part of the appeal of football to children. They delight in any chance to discharge aggressions and extra energy. Football has gentler attractions as well. The grace and the glory of making a terrific play, of running, jumping, and catching the ball holds universal appeal.

Everyone remembers the sensation of tearing down the field for that touchdown at least once. They know that they were unstoppable. It was glorious to feel the cold wind blasting their faces.

# The Smallest Kid on the Team

Jack was always the smallest kid in the neighborhood. The other kids let him join the football team, but most of the time he was completely ignored and never even allowed to carry the ball. Occasionally, however, they took pity on him and gave him a chance. The quarterback passed Jack the ball and all the big guys would block while he ran down the field for a touchdown. The exhilaration Jack felt during those moments tided him over through the lonely passive games, until his next chance came.

# The Untraditional Game

Just as in other games, children become inventive when conditions aren't suitable for a traditional football game. Often, there aren't enough kids on the block to make up a regulation team, so one child has to wear many hats. Obstacles have to be overlooked—as well as shortcomings of the playing field.

Eric and his friends used to bundle up and play football in the snow! There were enormous mounds of snow in the way and the kids pretended they were blockers. Of course, there was the additional challenge of simply scooping the ball up off the ground before it completely disappeared under the snow.

*Boy Making Football Tackle (1925)*   35

# Football Heroes

Football also provides an opportunity for children to fantasize about and emulate their favorite heroes. They become Steve Largent catching a magnificent touchdown pass, Walter Payton breaking a tackle and running ninety-nine yards for a touchdown, Johnny Unitas setting up to make a long pass, or Alan Ameche bursting into the end zone to win the NFL championship in sudden-death overtime. Football is truly a unique game because it combines ruggedness with grace. It can be both ugly and beautiful, physical and ethereal.

*Punt, Pass & Kick Competition (1955)* 37

# The Hoop Game

Basketball is another popular wintertime sport. The basketball net, suspended high off the ground, serves as a yardstick for a child's growth. Each fall, that net seems to have moved just a little closer to the ground!

Basketball can be played indoors, in school gyms, community centers, and YMCAs. It can also be played outdoors, since baskets can be tacked onto barns, garages, telephone poles, fences, trees—virtually anywhere. If a real basketball net isn't available, children invent one. Five-gallon paint cans, tires, and garbage cans do double duty as baskets. Tennis balls, sponges, or rolled-up socks are put to use as basketballs as well.

One such inventive youngster leaned his father's ladder against the barn. He practiced shooting a ball between the rungs of the ladder, starting at the bottom and working his way to the top. This game whiled away many hours on the farm.

# The Court

Unlike baseball and football, basketball can be played in a small space as well as in a large one. Children can transform the tiniest alley or driveway into a basketball court, with baskets hung from poles or garage doors.

Children enjoy playing basketball both in groups and alone. Long, solitary afternoons are filled up shooting baskets again and again, or practicing tricky dribbles. Playing with a group brings different challenges—as well as companionship and competition. Basketball always fills one with energy and releases tension. It almost feels like cheating to do something is so healthy, yet so much fun!

*Four Boys on a Sled* (1919)

39

# Winter Sports

Winter brings still more free-spirited delights to children, with such sports as sledding. Every town has its own "Big Hill," where children gather after a night's snowfall.

Dragging the sled over to the hill and finding every other child in town already there started off the best sledding adventures. Everyone loved and feared the speed whizzing down the hill. It was a challenge both to stay on the sled and avoid bumping into other children. At the bottom, it was a relief to make it down still in one piece. Everyone climbed up to speed down again and again. That long, slow trudge up the hill made the short, fast ride down even more of a thrill.

It was fun to see how many kids could pile onto one sled. The biggest kid always ended up on the bottom, which was the best place because he got to steer . . . but the littlest kid on top always ended up falling off.

# Graceful Gliders

As soon as the neighborhood pond froze, out came the figure skaters and ice hockey players. Any small pond nearby almost always froze in the wintertime. Each winter, parents accompanied children there to throw big stones at the ice to see whether the ice had frozen enough for skating.

City kids rarely had a nearby pond, but they enjoyed both indoor and outdoor skating rinks. They never had to worry about whether the ice was solid enough. Around and around in circles they'd skate, the music playing merrily in the background.

Norman
Rockwell

*Skating Race (1920)*

41

# Ice Sports

Like swimming, ice sports offer children an opportunity to test their skills in a different arena. These sports provide a chance to go faster, yet feel more graceful than is possible on the ground. Of course, ice supplies a chance for children to invent still more new games.

*Boy Skating (1914)*

Before a child feels really comfortable on ice skates, roller skates are always an option. A child watches the big kids play ice hockey. How fast they slid by! At home, rollerskating up and down the sidewalk and pretending to play ice hockey was another inventive game. An old golf club served as the stick and a ball as the puck. When more friends joined the game, things could get quite rough.

# A New Hockey Game

It was easier to be even more inventive when one was a little older. The group came up with a version of ice hockey using sticks and flat stones that had been collected all fall. There were no goals: the object of this game was just to keep the stone and themselves moving . . . fast!

In winter sports, children master the elements. This gives them a sense of accomplishment that they carry through into other aspects of their lives. Each season offers activities and challenges peculiar to it alone, and children have always delighted in this variety of settings.

# Growing Up with Sports

And so the year goes. Baseball, swimming, football, basketball, and sledding are woven together into the fabric of childhood. For children, the ritual of sports imparts a joyful order to their world. With each new baseball or football season comes the promise of the future, as each child comes to run even faster, jump even higher, and reach even farther.

*What Do You Teach a Boy of Twelve? (1955)*

# Chapter 2
# The Family and Sports

## Sports and Family Life

From the moment parents first try to teach their baby to catch a ball, sports and family life become intertwined. Parents work on developing their young child's hand-eye coordination by teaching the child to use a bat or a plastic racket. They are beginning to develop the child's interest in sports as well. Children are exposed to their parents' favorite sports in many ways. They are taken to the tennis court in strollers to watch their parents play. They are taken to a professional ball game with the family, and they listen to endless dinnertime conversations focusing on sports. Parents and older children, who often don't share many interests, find some common ground by rooting for the same team, or enjoying the same sport. Sports play an important role in family life, by providing a framework in which families can share with each other, reach each other, and sometimes challenge each other.

# Family Sports

Childhood recollections of family life center on sports in many families. Backyard baseball games with Mom, Dad, and brother come to mind. Sunday afternoons with the whole family gathered around the television set, munching popcorn, yelling with frustration at an inept football team repeat themselves generation after generation. Sultry summer evenings, sandwiched between parents at the ballpark, knowing bedtime was long ago, provide memories to last a lifetime.

The family at the tennis courts, hitting the ball back and forth to each other over the net are building memories. Someone would bounce balls for the littlest players to try to hit. Those were the times the family really seemed close.

Outside in the backyard, father shows an eager youngster how to hit a ball. The youngsters pitch to him; he hits the ball, and they field it. Sometimes several kids gathered to play, and father would alternate hitting to each. It always seemed so amazing that father could hit that ball no matter where it was thrown, and he could control exactly where the ball went. He would run after bad pitches, sticking out his bat with one hand, and the ball would still go exactly where he wanted it.

# Dad's Sports

Some fathers' sports were baseball and football. They probably played those sports well in school, and still followed them avidly as a fan. Others were more interested in lacrosse and soccer. Sometimes father would go outside to kick the ball with the neighborhood youngsters. He usually ended up falling or he would try to catch the lacrosse ball and miss. It made him angry that he couldn't play as well as he had when he was young, but he tried hard. He was always there rooting for everyone on the local teams. Perhaps father sometimes felt like the man pictured in Norman Rockwell's April fool spoof.

*April Fool: Fishing (1945)*

# Family Interests

Sports activity within families can take many forms. Usually, parents introduce their children to sports that have held a lifelong interest for them. With the introduction of sports comes the transference of life's lessons from parent to child: "You have to concentrate." "Keep your eyes on the ball." "Have confidence in yourself." "You have to work hard to be a winner." There is a timelessness to sports, as generations of parents continue to share the same wisdoms with their children. These early days of training are an important part of the bonding process between parent and child, and a way to make a child feel he or she is capable of anything.

# Mom and Baseball

Many mothers played baseball. Sometimes she was the pitcher, and she would try to throw the ball so that each child couldn't help but come in contact with it. If they missed, she would apologize for throwing a bad pitch. "Oops," she'd say, "that pitch was much too high." Or, "You couldn't possibly have hit that pitch—it was way outside." Nobody ever struck out; she would keep pitching until everyone got a hit. When the littlest players got a hit, mother would pretend to try very hard to tag them out, but they always managed to get a home run. Mothers had softer hearts and a different perspective of the game than fathers.

*Little Leaguer (1954)*

# Lifting Weights

Perhaps father lifted weights to keep in shape, and many youngsters tried to measure their progress toward adulthood by how much those

*Strength in Reserve (1973)*

weights would budge. Sometimes father would help boost the barbell over his child's head, letting the youngster feel, of course, that he was doing the bulk of the work himself. The young strongman would run bragging to mother about how much weight he lifted, and she would compliment him on being so big and strong.

*The Theatrical Sensation of Springtime (1920)*

# A Plethora of Sports

Families spend time together participating in many sports activities, such as bowling, bicycling, skiing, skating, hiking, sailing, fishing, and swimming. Sports are unequaled in their ability to appeal to all generations, and they foster a feeling of closeness among family members participating in them. Sports also provide a natural arena for the combination of camaraderie and competition inherent in a sibling relationship. Older children are alternately patient with and frustrated by their younger siblings' attempts to play a game. Younger children, envious when older siblings bring home their first lacrosse stick or real baseball glove, push to match the skills of their brothers and sisters. Siblings challenge each other, even as they root for each other. They also are pals, who find pleasure in playing together on neighborhood teams, or inventing new versions of sports to play with each other.

Brothers loved to throw tennis balls against basement doors and practice catching them in their baseball gloves. The game was made more exciting by the family pet. She adored tennis balls and could keep two balls in her mouth at once, one in each cheek. First she would retrieve one ball, drop it, and wait for a second ball. After she got the second ball, she would go back and stuff the first ball in her mouth too. The challenge for the ball throwers was to catch the ball before the dog got it. If they missed the ball, she would pounce on it and run down the yard to stockpile it with her other balls. They could then take a different ball from her pile and play with it until a catch was missed and the dog absconded with the ball once again.

If there were a lot of children in the neighborhood, they played baseball and football together with teams made up of brothers and sisters, of all ages. There was usually a family with at least seven kids, so they almost filled up a team by themselves. Some siblings were close in age and the younger one always wanted to do everything the elder did. Playing neighborhood sports together allowed this competition.

# Vacations

Family vacations offered chances to participate in different sports than were usually possible back home. Many families went to the beach for two weeks every summer. Usually there was no lifeguard at the beach, and mother was always worried that the children might get caught in the surf. So the whole family would go in the water together and keep an eye on each other. Fine times were had by all, floating past each other and rolling over the waves. Diving under the huge waves, the family immediately looked up and checked to make sure that everyone was still there. No one ever went swimming in the surf themselves; it was purely a family event.

*Swimming in the Surf (1961)*

53

# Fishing Adventures

Fishing was an outlet for fathers who were not interested in active sports. Fishing vacations in the mountains were major events. Every year, he'd promise that soon his children would be old enough to go out fishing with him for the day. They first needed to learn how to be still, he said, and to have more patience. The children carried this promise around for quite some time before the day finally came when father offered to take someone with him. They woke up early in the morning, going out when the air was still cool over the lake. The motor boat was eased quietly out to the middle of the lake and father and child sat quietly, not saying a word. The dragonflies hovered and sat on the edge of the fishing poles. At lunchtime, sandwiches were unpacked that mother made and were eaten in the boat. Father and child stayed out on the lake all day, only occasionally catching a fish. It was a quiet, reflective time to share with father, and the child felt more like a companion. As a special treat, Dad would allow the privileged one run the motorboat on the way home.

Other families were very sports-minded, and were always involved in a lot of activities together. For some reason, the times that remain crystal-clear are the vacations when the family tried something new, with little success. One such mishap occurred during a family vacation at the beach. Grandpop describes such a time. He remembers renting a small boat and some fishing gear. He rowed everyone out into the bay to wait for the fish to bite. They waited in vain, for that day there was very little fish action. Each person would get very excited when they felt a strong tug on the line, but soon found out that what they had caught was a rather large turtle, or a log, or some other trash. The climax of the day usually occurred when a rented pole dropped into the water and could not be retrieved. The boat was steered to the shore, the lost pole paid for and fishing was not a part of the agenda for the remaining vacation.

This could also happen during the family vacation at a lake. A cabin was rented for the weekend. The family also rented a motorboat to explore the lake, and somewhere that seemed to be the exact center of the lake, the motor slipped overboard. The fishing pole incident of a few years earlier reminded the family that rented motorboats represented a certain measure of trouble for them. Perhaps they should be avoided at all costs!

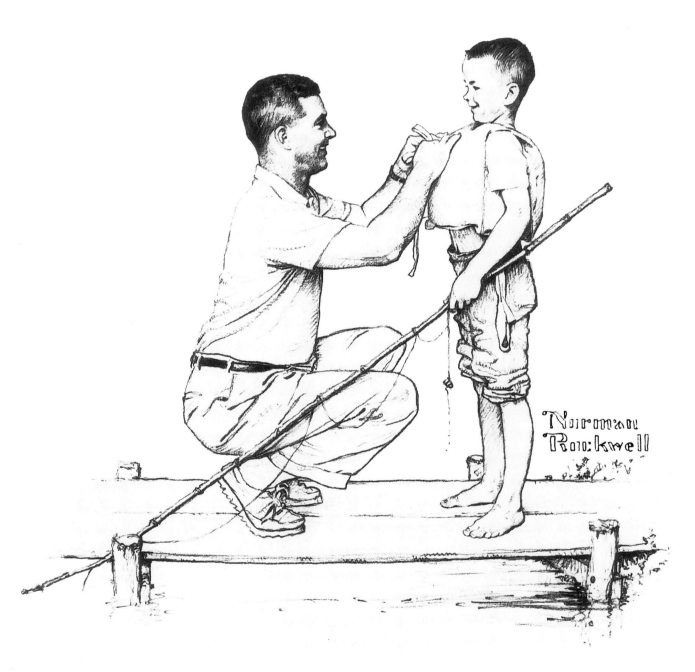

*Boy and Dad on Dock (1960)*

# A Sailing Adventure

Daunted in their attempts with a motorboat, the family decided to take up sailing. From the lakeside cottage, everyone watched the colorful sails of sunfishes float by, and longed to be out there catching the breeze, also. Father said that he had been on many sailboats with friends and was sure that he knew enough about sailing to attempt a short ride. So off the family went, with what turned out to be virtually no knowledge of what to do. First father swung the boom around so fast that it narrowly missed decapitating someone and, throwing the boat off balance, tipped the boat over. Everyone got an unexpected dunking. That usually convinced everyone to stick to landlocked sports in which they had some competency.

*Pride-O-Body (1916)*   57

# Winter Sports

Winter sports provide fond family memories. Learning to ski together was a memorable occasion. The children started out skiing on a large hill at a friend's house. Several families would congregate on the hill each time it snowed. They would spend the day skiing down the hill and trudging back up since, of course, there was no lift. Then someone would extend the invitation for hot chocolate, and an uproarious party continued the family fun. As the family became better skiers, they would go away together to a ski resort. This lasted until mother broke her leg on an icy slope and decided she was perhaps too old to take up a new sport.

Family sledding was a special treat. Every family had at least two sleds; brother and mother would pile on one, and father and sister on the other. Father insisted on steering, mother would share the chore. Whoever rode with father just held on as tightly as possible.

# Vacation Sports

A family vacation to relatives in the city furnished a new playing field and new participants. Baseball-playing experience, up to that point, was limited to a backyard, where a well-hit ball would land on the neighbor's side of the fence or become lost in the ivy. In the city, there was a regulation baseball diamond in the park. The family reunion may only provide 4 or 5 players on each team, but it was enough to seem as though the teams were playing real baseball for the first time. Someone would suggest spending the entire vacation at that baseball diamond, but unfortunately they were the minority voice.

Thanksgiving at an aunt's house in the country was a surprise for an inactive family. The visiting family was accustomed to spending Thanksgiving day watching football and consuming large quantities of food. They were surprised and exhausted by how this larger and more active family spent their day. Cousins by marriage were large both in number and height. The first thing to try was hiking and rock climbing in a nearby park. That done, it was home to shoot a few baskets and play some football. After all the activities, the Thanksgiving dinner was a relief.

# Spectators and Participants

If one came from a large, very athletic family, a repertoire of sporting skills were soon acquired. Family gatherings always involved a game. They weren't that competitive because cousins of all ages joined in; they were just fun. Sports represented a cheerful family time.

Families can enjoy sports together as spectators and as participants. Many families spend time together watching games on television or listening on the radio. Many families attend sports events together, enjoying the feeling of being together in a crowd, of cheering for the same team.

# The First Ball Game

Most people can remember that classic rite of childhood, the first time their parents took them to the ballpark. A sunny but cool Sunday afternoon seemed to be the most opportune time for a baseball outing. The family chose seats in the lower stands, behind home plate. Under cover, it was surprisingly cold, and the fans were bundled up in layers of clothing. Heavy sweatshirts and the baseball cap just bought at the concession stand helped, but the people under cover were still cold. Below, in the box seats, people were basking in the sun in short-sleeved shirts. The littlest child sat on father's lap, even though she had her own seat, so she could see over the people in the row in front. Everyone held their hats to their chest, just like the players on the field, when the *Star–Spangled Banner* was played.

Baseball always was an exciting game and parents and children were both yelling and cheering, eating hot dogs and peanuts together. The home team won, and the exhilarating feeling stayed with everyone the rest of the evening. Someone always put their ticket stub in a special-things box to keep for always. It had been such a great feeling, parents and children joined in successfully cheering on the team. No one wanted the day to end.

When father took one child to see the first professional baseball game of their young lives, it was an extra special treat. Father knew the team inside and out, and kept up a running commentary as each player came up to bat. It was surprising that father, who was a shy person, talked to everyone in the stands. Perhaps this was the first time the child noticed how sports could bring the oddest people together. There was father chatting away with strangers, as if he had known them all his life. Often the child didn't know what was more impressive; being in a ballpark for the first time or catching a glimpse of the sociable man, at ease with the crowd, who was father.

*Crossed Signals (1913)*

# A Basketball Weekend

Parents were big college basketball fans. When the final rounds of a basketball tournament were held at a nearby college, families would spend the entire weekend attending one game after the other. Eyes would be stinging by the end of the day from the smoke hovering in the field house. The youngsters were in awe of all the college kids cheering for their schools.

# The Fifty Yard Line

Lucky children had parents with season tickets on the fifty yard line to professional football games. Occasionally, mother wouldn't want to go to the game, and father alternately took sister or brother in her place. It was a treat to go to the game with father. Because he had sat in the same seats for years, he knew everyone in the stands for rows in front of and behind his seats. "So this is your daughter," his stadium acquaintances would say, and they gently teased her throughout the game. The woman in front had a cow bell and would ring it loudly each time the home team made a good play. Mother sent along thermoses of hot tea for father and hot chocolate for the child. There was a stadium blanket to throw across knees to keep warm. Father would yell and groan at the plays, but the child just sat and soaked up the sounds and smells of the game.

# The Luck of the Game

Local newspapers sometimes sponsored a contest that required guessing which players would make the team for the American and National leagues, and the batting order. The prize was two tickets to the game. Fathers and children sat down together and came up with a lineup for both teams. The lucky family got all the players right and made only one mistake on the batting order. They won the tickets! The newspaper had a picture of them, holding up their tickets. The lucky family got a ball autographed by the all-star catcher. This memory became one of the most exciting experiences of childhood.

# Dinner Discussions

Sports sometimes enters family life by way of the dinner table. Mealtime conversations often concerned the virtues or ills of the local teams, comparisons of present-day players with the all-time greats, children discussing their successes that day on the field at school, or parents reminiscing about their own childhood sports successes.

When parents were good athletes, and had achieved some national recognition, dinner table conversations often involved reminiscences of past successes, or stories about sports "the way they used to be." Mother liked to talk about when she was in the hockey Olympics, an event that was held before hockey was included in the regular Olympics. Father had colorful baseball stories to tell.

His picture hung on the wall of the den and he was always ready to talk about his baseball career. He was a good pitcher, and the Boston Red Sox and Philadelphia A's had both tried unsuccessfully to sign him. He wasn't attracted to the life of a ballplayer, in particular the long, hot bus rides. But he was hired sometimes to pitch batting practice for the pros because his arm was so accurate.

Father always talked about what a talented and spunky quarterback he'd been even though he was very small and slight. His nose had been broken a couple times, he said, by bravely plowing through his opponents, who were always twice his size.

Baseball was the main topic of conversation in many houses at the dinner table. No matter what player was discussed, father always ended up bragging about what a great player he himself had been. He'd played second base for a Class B team out west. One day a child came across a minor league record book and looked up the record. Much to everyone's surprise, father had been a better than average player.

Sisters and brothers all played team sports. By the time the family sat down for dinner, chances were that somebody in the family had been in a game that day. The topic of conversation at dinner usually was about that game, and father, who considered himself a sports expert, gave commentary and criticism about how the children played.

In many families, talk revolved around sports. In the morning, father would read the sports pages out loud. "How about those Yankees, they've changed managers again." "Why did Robinson play that bum at first base again; he can't hit or field, I don't know why they keep him in." At the dinner table, he would lecture on the best athletes who ever played, and then quiz everyone to make sure they had absorbed his information.

*The Indian Sign (1916)*

# The Sports Connection

Sports can not only connect parent with child, but also grandparents with grandchildren. Grandfather talked incessantly about what a terrific hitter he'd been on his school baseball team, and how he was sure he could still slug that ball. "After all," he'd say, "In 1963, Stan Musial hit a home run in his first at bat after becoming a grandfather." One day, the entire family went to the park for a picnic and baseball game. Grandpa came up to bat and Dad shouted, "Show them what you can do." He swung and missed twice, then looked rather worried. "Hope I haven't lost my stuff," he muttered. On the third pitch, he smoked a hit to right field. He asked his fastest grandson to pinch run for him, because his legs were a bit rusty. Grandpa and Grandson gave each other a high five as they changed places on the base.

Grandfather always talked about how he practically grew up on ice skates. The pond close to his house remained frozen all winter, and he and his friends played ice hockey and competed to see whose footwork was fanciest. One day, he offered to take everyone skating and "show them a thing or two." He was a great showman. The neighborhood kids stopped skating and watched him whirl around. He made the family very proud.

*Gramps Skating (1921)*

# Summer Sports with Grandpa

Summers were spent visiting Grandpa, who lived on a mountain. There was a pond on his property, which he stocked with fish every year. At 5 a.m., Grandpa would wake anyone he could to go fishing with him. They would trudge across the wet grass, through low-hanging, misty clouds, to the pond. Everything smelled damp and pine-scented. Little frogs hopped into the water as they walked through the grass near the water. Grandpa showed how to bait the hook with worms, or sometimes with bacon, and cast the line into the water and wait for the fish to bite. Everyone would sit there in silent companionship for the rest of the morning.

Fishing with grandfather, playing football with brother in the backyard, walking hand in hand with father to the ballpark for the first time; these are old rituals that span the generations, and that connect the children of fifty years ago to the children of today.

*Gramps at the Plate (1916)*

*Football Hero (1938)*

# Chapter 3
# Sports Fans

## The Fans

Many people are involved with sports as fans. They cheer for their school teams, they frequent professional sport games, they spend their leisure time watching sports on television or listening on the radio. Fans range from diehard fanatics to casual spectators. Some become personally involved in the sport as cheerleaders, referees, or umpires.

For some fans, sports are a way to relax at the end of the day. To them, watching sports on television or listening to the radio is calming. They trade the conflicts of their lives for the impermanent conflicts of the game.

For other fans, however, sports are most important. The outcome of a game can affect their morale for days afterwards. These fans are as involved in the sport as are the players. They identify closely with the team and are consumed by their passion. They might fill their house with team memorabilia, and memorize every detail about the roster. They plan vacations to follow their team to spring training. They wait at the airport in the early hours of the morning for the team to arrive home after a losing road trip. The emotional ups and downs of their life coincide with the successes of their team.

# Baseball Fans

Baseball inspires the same fanaticism. Each time a fan goes to the ballpark to see a baseball game, they still feel the same excitement that they did when they were kids. The stadium may be an old one, standing on borrowed time, or a new, modern park, but it is as comfortable as an old shoe. Year after year, the avid fan parks the car on the same side street each time and waves to the people sitting on their stoops. He enters the stadium through the same gate, to his seats near third base, over the dugout. The crowd always looks sparse at first, but continues to fill up, even into the third inning. The lineups are announced, the visiting team roundly booed, the home team cheered. The crowd rises for *The Star–Spangled Banner*, the umpire shouts "Play Ball," and everyone loses themselves for the next two or three hours in the universe of "The Game."

Being a spectator also means buying hot dogs and from the vendors, talking baseball with the people sitting next to you, and getting caught up in the emotions of the crowd. Traditions are important, like hearing the same song every year during the seventh-inning stretch. Trying to change songs causes great consternation among the crowd. After the home team wins, the crowd stands and cheers, not wanting to go home.

*Hundredth Year of Baseball* (1939)     73

# Family Football Fans

Family season football tickets mean the family has sat in the same section at the stadium for generations. Since football is only played once a week, it seems to be more of a special event than baseball, which is played almost every day. The family has Sunday friends there, people they don't know personally but whom they've seen go through marriages, divorces, and pregnancies. The people in front of the family used to bring their kids to the game; now their grandchildren come also. There is the lady who always comes to the game in high heels, and the man who balances 14 hot dogs and 16 hot chocolates and somehow still makes it to his seat.

Football fans are fanatics. They scream and yell a lot, and are great believers in their team. The fans seem to enjoy the physical aspects of the game, the on-field collisions, and the excitement of the seconds on the clock ticking away. Being part of the crowd pumps one up; the enthusiasm is contagious.

# Basketball Fans

A rabid basketball fan will say he doesn't know why it bothers him so much, but he's depressed for days after a big loss. When his team loses with 5 seconds left in the game, he couldn't believe it. Even after seeing the instant replay about 5 times, he still hopes the ending would be different. He keeps thinking, "Maybe this time, the other team will miss the shot."

Sometimes it's hard to separate one's enjoyment of the sport itself from the pleasure of being out at the stadium or arena. It is not just the game but the total experience of watching a game that is important to a fan.

# Fans and Losing

When the team loses, the spirits of the fans suffer too. Fans feel euphoric after wins, dejection after losses, tension during big games. They jeer at players they feel are not giving their all. They berate umpires and referees whose calls go against their teams. Fans, particularly those of sports such as tennis and golf, get very involved in the personalities of the athletes. Many of them play the sport themselves for pleasure and, therefore, have great respect for the talents of the players.

# Golf Fans

Many fans enjoy golf because it is such a civilized sport. There are no owners and players unions, no multi-million dollar salaries. Golfers get paid according to their performance in each tournament. There is no roughness, and everything is done on the honor system. Most fans watching a tournament are knowledgeable about golf and have a great love for the game.

*Golf Tip (1960)*

# How a Fan Grows

Life as a fan often begins during school days. Students begin attending school basketball, football, and hockey games more for social reasons than for sports enjoyment, but "The Game" soon becomes the thing.

Many become ardent basketball fans in high school. Some girls start going to games because of a crush on one of the players. They soon find that there is something emotionally contagious, almost seductive, about cheering a team to victory. A few friends meet at school and ride the bus with the team to their games. Even the shy and reserved love to go to the games and scream. It is the only place where they feel free to let go and yell, and lose themselves in the crowd. They get caught up in being part of a team and in the competitiveness of it and begin to care if the team wins or loses.

Girls sometimes first want to be a cheerleader because it is the thing to be. When they are in front of the crowd, they get emotionally involved. It uses up a lot of energy, pumping up the crowd, staying upbeat even when the team is losing badly. Then, every season, there's that one important game, perhaps it's Homecoming or when the team is playing its arch rival. It's a close game with the score going back and forth, but finally the home team loses. The cheerleaders sit on the basketball court afterwards with the other cheerleaders and just sob. They root so hard for the team that the outcome of the game matters. Knowing the players so well makes them feel doubly sorry for them when they lose a big game. It is amazing how school spirit is so often tied to the sports successes of the school. It's easy to feel proud when you're on top.

The school pep club sat in a section in the bleachers, and cheered along with cheerleaders. The pep club members wore special shirts that were one color on one side and another on the other. All sorts of interesting formations were worked out with these colors. The pep club members and the crowd got so absorbed in the game. Everyone got so caught up in the cheering, that they felt completely wrung out at the end of the game.

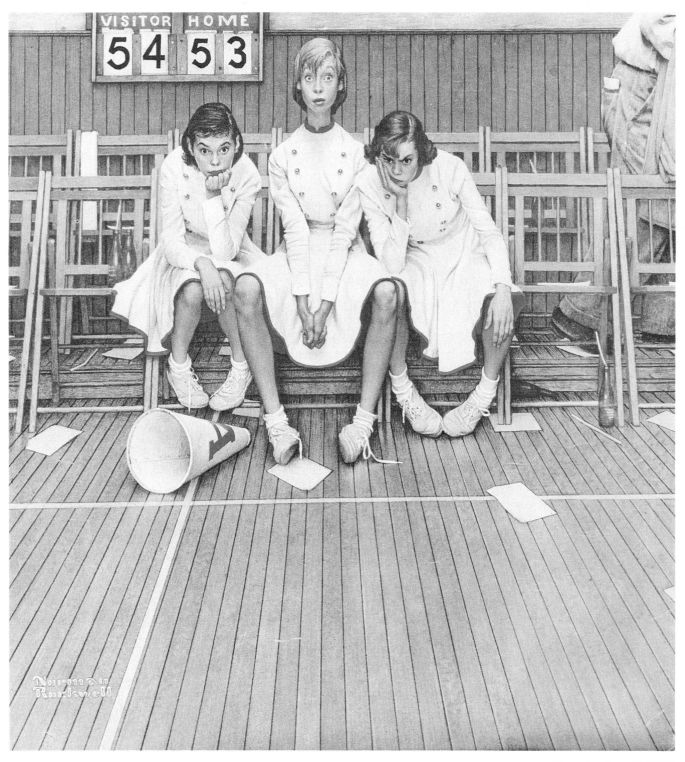

*Cheerleaders (1952)*

# Becoming a Game Official

When a fan wants even more personal involvement in a sport, they may choose to become an umpire or referee. When they stop playing sports, they still find they want to be involved on a more personal level than just being a spectator in the stands. The pay isn't much, so most referees are people who love the sport.

They travel from school to school, sometimes calling two games in a day. They take a yearly test to keep their accreditation current.

Umpire's camp is an opportunity to work on getting a national rating. This rating is the highest award an umpire or referee can acquire. Being a referee is a great way to see games while still being involved on the field.

*The Referee (1950)*

# Professional Status

Many dreamed about playing professional baseball and about growing up to be the second Babe Ruth. When the movie "The Babe Ruth Story" came to local movie theaters, children would go in when the theater opened in the afternoon, and leave after the last show, if they were allowed to stay.

Willie Mays was another hero. His fans always tried to emulate his famous basket catch. His box scores were followed religiously, and the number 24 appeared on many jerseys. Hank Aaron caused many an argument in many families. At night, when brothers were supposed to be sleeping, they argued about their choices for the greatest player. One maintained that Hank Aaron was better because his lifetime average was higher; but the other argued that Willie Mays was a better fielder. This argument would continue until father came in and threatened dire consequences if everyone did not immediately go to sleep.

The ghosts of other games played in other years lurk in every playing field. Every fan has a game or an experience etched in his mind.

Father recalled going to double headers in the early twenties. The fans would go in to the stadium to see the first game. They then left to stand in line to get tickets for the second game.

Every year, some major league teams used to barnstorm on their way up from Florida. Their last exhibition game was always against a minor league team. During the game, the Orioles hit a routine fly ball to Joe DiMaggio, who dropped it. It was probably the only fly ball he had dropped since elementary school. After that, people used to say, "Joe DiMaggio . . . I saw him drop a fly ball; he isn't so great."

A tennis fan remembers the first time he ever saw the big serve in tennis. The football fan remembers the Hail Mary pass in the final seconds that won the game. The baseball fan remembers the no-hit game by one of the great pitchers.

Or the game might have been memorable because it gave the fan a chance to see his hero in person, or an important playoff game. Or perhaps a game is memorable because it was unusually well played and unusually exciting.

*Red Sox Locker Room* (1957)

# Sports Ideals

Some fans love sports indiscriminately. Most fans reserve their passion for one particular sport, and one particular team.

Families usually choose their favorite team from the teams and sports in the area where they live. When the team moves, father may transfer his allegiance to another team. Mother and children may be influenced enough by father not to root for the transplanted team, so they pick their own favorite teams.

Choices are made sometimes because of a favorite player. This made things very interesting in the household, with everyone rooting for a different team. Perhaps the opposing teams met each other in the playoffs for the pennant and it was a close game into the final innings. The person who chose the winning team felt some sort of stature by being the only one to have backed the winning team.

Many fans have a favorite player whose career they follow closely and whose playing style they try to emulate. The fantasies of young fans revolve around their sports heroes, and they willingly shift their allegiance to another team if their hero is traded.

# Excitement at the Game

One of the most exciting football games was the game when the Baltimore Colts beat the New York Giants in a sudden-death playoff at Yankee Stadium. The Colts were on their own 14 yard line, with only 1:56 left in the game, and they were losing 17-14. Unitas started firing passes to Raymond Berry, and began moving the team down the field. With only about a minute to play, the Colts were still only at mid-field. Unitas kept on completing passes to Berry, who set a playoff game record for the most receptions. With only 9 seconds left on the clock, Steve Myhra place kicked a 20-yard field goal, tying the score at 17 to 17. The game then went into sudden death overtime. The Giants started out with the ball, but they were forced to punt. Then the Colts started to move the ball. The crowd noise was deafening. It had gotten dark and frosty cold outside, and the stadium lights were on. When Alan Ameche plunged into the end zone for a touchdown, giving the Colts a 23-17 victory, Colt fans went wild. People stood in the stands, applauding and cheering. Others spilled onto the field and were going crazy, jumping around and ripping apart the grass. The Colts Band marched up and down the field playing the Colts fight song. The celebration seemed to go on forever. Nobody wanted to go home, nobody even wanted to stop the loud, loud celebration. Everyone chased away the cold and the tension of the close game with their exuberance.

The rabid fan who was at home had a different viewpoint. He was watching the game on television, when the television picture went off during the overtime period. Apparently, when some fans rushed on the field to watch the action from the sidelines, they accidentally disconnected a power cable. The agonized fan started flipping channels to check if his set was still functioning. He was so caught up in the tension of the game that he felt like exploding with frustration when the picture went. He quickly turned on the radio in the kitchen, and ran back and forth from kitchen to living room, checking to see if the television picture had returned. After a couple minutes, the picture returned, in time to see Ameche crossing the goal line for the winning touchdown. That situation can give the fan an extra jolt of adrenalin.

# Parents as Fans

Sometimes it is their child's participation in a sport that turns parents into sports fans. As their children appear in baseball, soccer, and lacrosse leagues and swimming meets, play tennis matches, and participate in school basketball and football games, parents become the most dedicated of fans. They spend their weekends and late-spring weekday evenings watching their child practice and compete. Sometimes, they travel around the country so their child can compete on a national level. They are the loudest cheerers in the bleachers, sometimes the most loyal fans and sometimes the most vocal critics.

There is nothing to match the feeling of pride and tension of watching your child compete in a sport. You want so much for him to do well, for the team to do well. You worry that he will get injured, or make a big mistake. You know most of the team members personally, and feel happy for them when they make a good play. The outcome of the game seems less important than the individual achievements of your child and his friends.

Father usually came to all the games to root for his child and the team. After each game, he always gave advice about what had been wrong and what had been right. Sometimes he wasn't very familiar with the sport, and his comments were usually far afield. He would drive some of the team home—there were usually 8 or 10 kids in the car—and if they lost that day he would tell them what was done wrong. He always seemed to be giving the wrong criticism at the wrong time. Other than his own child, the other kids never took offense at his criticism. They were just happy for the ride home.

Mother usually managed to attend the games also. She came to all the games and sat on the sidelines, usually without saying much. At the end of the game, she commented either "You played well," or "You didn't play so well." One game, when she thought her child was about to make a mistake, she screamed at her from the sidelines. This so shocked her daughter that she missed the play. Mothers generally were quieter fans than fathers.

*Son's Football Game (1950)*

# Cheers and Jeers

Sports fans have very strong likes and dislikes. Each has a favorite sport, a favorite team, a favorite stadium, and a favorite player. Often, the fan also has a most hated team. Each fan also has a singular style to cheer a favorite team. Some like to watch with quiet appreciation, others like to let themselves go and yell and scream.

Grandfather always tells a story about the time he went to a football game, and a man sat right behind him with an air horn. Grandfather sat there, bearing up under the noise of the air horn blaring in his ear, as long as he could stand it. Finally, he offered the man ten dollars for the horn. The man wouldn't sell it, he was having too much fun with it. A little while later, Grandfather offered $25 for the horn. The man still wouldn't sell. Finally, after an hour of listening to the air horn, grandfather says, "I'll give you a hundred dollars for that stupid horn." Then the man sold him the air horn and Grandfather enjoyed the end of the football game.

In the late thirties, the Davis Club matches were played in Philadelphia. Australia was playing the United States. Back then, one kept very quiet at tennis matches. Every time someone made a good shot, one man would yell at the top of his lungs, "Go, you Jackie," or "Go, you Bobby." Finally, the man was ousted from the game, having violated the tennis protocol of the thirties.

Whether noisy or quiet, relaxed or tense, fans have one thing in common—they love sports. True fans feel a closeness with their sport and identify closely with their team or favorite players. They feel a sense of loss when their team loses, or moves to another city. They feel exuberant when they've backed a winner. Through sports, fans develop a feeling of identity and pride, a feeling of belonging to a school, a team, or even a city.

*Absent Treatment (1917)*  89

*Casey at the Bat (1970)*

# Chapter 4
# Meeting The Challenge

## A Personal Challenge

Jim Abbott was born with only one arm, and pitches major league ball for the California Angels. It is clear that he set a personal challenge for himself a long time ago, and that he has met that challenge. This is a dramatic example of how people can challenge themselves as athletes. However, all people who participate in sports, at all ages and at all levels, feel the challenge to compete and excel. To them, the development of their talent and the process of the game matters as much as the outcome.

Dad remembers, "There were two things I was good at when I was young: running and jumping. I used to practice jumping over anything that was in my way—the lawn mower, a saw horse, a bush. I was always challenging myself to jump over new things, which was scary because many times I wasn't sure I could do it. I usually made the jump, however, and then pushed myself to try jumping over even taller objects."

"I was one of the smallest and most puny kids in my class, but I was well-coordinated and wanted to be able to compete with the other kids in sports. So I started lifting weights and running to get myself in condition. I remember checking myself out in the mirror to see how much my muscles were developing. I kept challenging myself to go one step further, to lift just a little more weight, to run just a little farther."

"Because of my favorite hero, I spent hours and hours practicing my fielding. Because of this I became a very strong fielder and always felt more at home in the outfield than I did at bat."

For some athletes, the goal is to win the big tournaments, to play on a championship team. For others, the goal is simply to achieve some measure of personal triumph.

On a softball team, right field is always where they put the weakest fielders. In other words, not many balls were hit to right field, so anybody could play there without much fielding ability. There comes a time, when there are two men on base, someone on the opposing team hits a screaming line drive to the right fielder. How glorious it is to make a diving shoestring catch. The other team, not expecting a catch, keeps on running. A perfect throw to second base, then on to first, is the stuff dreams are made of. This is a right fielder's perfect dream.

# The Track Team

In our very small school, the track coach needed to recruit thirteen people for the track team. A large meet was coming up. Since thirteen of us, including myself, tried out for the team, we all were selected. There was no way I would have made the team if there had been more competition.

I went to work practicing wind sprints, getting in shape to run in the 100 meter and 200 meter race. My coach thought I should eat steak and eggs every morning, so every morning my mother made me steak and eggs. At the meet, I finished seventh out of twelve runners, which was something of a personal victory for me.

*The Purple Pennant (1916)*

# Pickup Games

Saturday pickup basketball games give the less than perfect player another chance to shine. Lack of skill can be canceled out by lack of age. Being ten years younger than the other players and having double their lung capacity is a distinct advantage.

One thing to learn is that you can be a winner even if you don't have the obvious physical attributes needed. Many football players are too small and too slow to be top quarterbacks, but they accomplish their goals. Anything is possible if you set goals for yourself and work hard to meet them.

*Four Sporting Boys: Basketball (1951)* 95

# The Coach

Uncle Jim coached a basketball team made up of some big 14 and 15 year old kids. The smallest kid on the court, who was 14, made a basket just as time was running out and won the game. He walked away feeling a lot better about himself.

There's usually at least one memorable game or sports-related experience in the life of an athlete. The experience can be for better or for worse.

# Street Sports

Living in an urban neighborhood, there were a lot of other teenagers around the same age. Street sports and hanging around gyms shooting baskets took up much leisure time.

The quarterback of the neighborhood football team had an interesting dilemma. They had no uniforms or organization to speak of, but somebody arranged for his team to play a game against the St. Katherine's Industrial School.

His team showed up at the appointed time and met with a team, fully uniformed. The players were two or three times as tall and as broad as his team was, or so it seemed to the quarterback. The street team lined up, with everyone feeling scared stiff.

The quarterback called all the plays, which usually consisted of handing the ball to someone and telling him to run either to the right or left. The ball was snapped, and the quarterback called the play. "Marshall, take the ball and run to the right." "Not me," said Marshall.

The quarterback was forced to run straight ahead himself. On the next play, the same thing happened. "Freddy," he said, "take the ball and run to the left." "Not me," said Freddy, and again the quarterback ran with the ball.

Needless to say, street teams didn't develop much offense. They didn't develop much defense, either, for that matter.

*The Ghost Ball (1914)*

# The Best Error

The other side of the coin is the game where a mistake wins the game. Grandfather describes such a game he played as a boy.

He was the first batter up that inning, and hit a triple to right field. It was in the eighth inning and his team was losing by a run.

The next batter up hit a soft grounder to second, and Grandfather held at third. One down. The next batter hit a sharp grounder and Grandfather started to run for home. Then he realized that the ball had gone straight to the second baseman, just like the grounder before it.

The second baseman threw home. There the ball was waiting for Grandfather in the catcher's mitt, with at least another ten feet for him to go to reach the plate. Thoughts whirled around in his head. "How could I have been so stupid, I am going to be the goat of this game." In a last-ditch, desperate attempt, he set his eye on the catcher's glove and ran right into it.

Miraculously, the ball popped out of the glove and rolled away. Grandfather doubled back and touched the plate again, just in case he had missed it before, and scored the tying run. The ball kept on rolling in foul territory, over on the first base side. His teammate who had hit the grounder ended up all the way on third base. He scored on a fly ball, and Grandfather's team ended up winning 3-1. Of course, it became his favorite story.

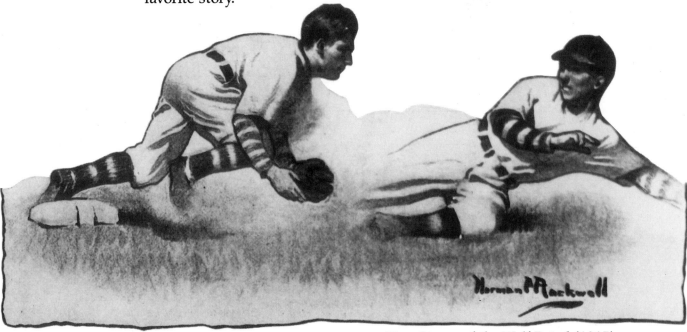

*Don Strong of the Wolf Patrol (1915)*

# Dad's Stories

Dad still remembers with painful clarity the hockey game when he missed two open goals against a team that should have been beaten easily. He winces when he tells the story about winning, because his team just barely won a game that should have been so easy.

Then he remembers the times when all the breaks went his way. His favorite story is about a lacrosse game he played in college. His ball hit the crossbar, then ricocheted to hit the goalie in the back of the head and score a goal.

*Your Own Hockey Rink (1914)*

Another time, playing soccer, he was walking away from the goal. The goalie threw out the ball and he did a scissors kick, catching the ball on the edge of his toe. He kicked it in for a goal.

His office is in a softball league. They were playing a game and were down by one run in the last inning. The bases were loaded, there were two outs, and the biggest hitter on Dad's team was up at bat. All he needed to do was get a hit, which he always did anyway, and the office would win. The heavy hitter swung at the pitch as hard as he could; the ball went up in the air and plopped down right on top of the plate. This fiasco has been the office joke ever since.

# The Big One

Nothing in life can ever approach the feeling of being successful in The Big Game. Hitting a triple off an unhittable pitcher, shooting the ball into the basket for the winning points with only 4 seconds left in the game or hitting the puck into the goal is a matchless thrill.

Uncle Jim remembers his college football team was losing 45-41 in a championship game. They had the ball on the 50 yard line with only 5 seconds left to play. The quarterback threw one final Hail Mary pass, which miraculously landed right in the hands of a team member. He sprinted the remaining yards into the end zone for a touchdown, and Uncle Jim's team won the game. The feeling of coming through with The Big One is an incomparable one. Fans rushed on the field, and everyone hugged everyone else with joy, sharing the victory with each other.

# Going the Wrong Way

The game that is never forgotten is one in which a goal is scored—unfortunately, in the wrong goal area. As the player runs down the field in the wrong direction, he must wonder why his teammates were not where they should be. The teammates are so stunned to see the ball carrier go the wrong way that they just stand there and stare.

The hapless ball carrier is so mortified that he wishes he were anywhere else, in any other business and laboring under an assumed identity. No matter what sports triumphs may be in store for this person in the future, he will forever remember the embarrassment of that mistake.

*Hitting the Line (1917)*

# A Personal Best

Many times, meeting a personal goal is more important than winning. Climbing a mountain or simply completing a marathon or long-distance bicycle race can be very satisfying achievements.

Uncle Jim took up running because, with his busy schedule, team sports were hard to schedule. He felt that running was the basis of all sports. So he started running every day, going about 40 or 50 miles a week.

The more he ran, the more he wanted to run. He set goals for himself. If he ran 5 miles a day last week, he tried to run 6 miles a day this week. The ultimate challenge, finally, was to run a marathon.

Winning was never a consideration. He just wanted to see if he could go the distance. Uncle Jim entered a marathon held locally and was surprised by how many of his friends came to cheer him on to the finish line. He remembers coming up to the finish line and feeling ready to give up, when he saw some of his friends. That pushed him on, and he finally finished with a time of 4 hours and a few seconds.

*The Fencer (1960)*

# Practice Makes Perfect

One goal of a sports participant is to improve skills by practicing and playing the game regularly.

At recess, I always joined a soccer game organized by kids two grades ahead of me. The team captains chose sides, and my friend and I were usually the last to be picked.

It didn't discourage me to play with bigger kids, who were better at playing the game. I learned by watching them play.

When I scored a goal, it meant even more to me because I'd beaten the big kids. I liked being out there on the field, running fast, and being a part of what was happening.

*Black Water Dave (1916)*

# Shooting Sports

Gun sports, too, are popular for the challenge they involve. Target shooting is man versus the target. It becomes a challenge for the shotgunner to see how many targets he can break without a miss, and to continue to top his own record. Hunters enjoy the challenge of outwitting a bird or animal.

# Sports Pals

While many people enjoy participating in sports for the challenge, others enjoy participating for the camaraderie.

Aunt Jill always enjoyed team sports better than individual sports. She liked the camaraderie of playing on a team, and not having all the pressure just on her.

One night a week, her co-workers meet to play softball or volleyball together. Playing together creates a friendly atmosphere, which carries over into the work place.

She played field hockey on her high-school team, and enjoyed the companionship of the other girls as much as she enjoyed playing. Sometimes, the coach would let the team members take the equipment home. They would go to someone on the team's house with sleeping bags and hockey equipment, and have a slumber party. In the morning, after breakfast, they would go into the yard and divide into small teams for a practice session. Aunt Jill treasured these memories.

# Racing Sports

Speed, defined as pushing yourself or your vehicle to the limits, seems to attract people to sports such as track and field, and car, bicycle, and motorcycle racing.

Dad encouraged my interest in racing starting with go-cart races when I was a kid. We built a go-cart with an old lawn mower engine and scraps of wood. I became impatient to try it, because it took most of the winter to build.

When it was finally ready, I took it out for a drive. It was really fast, but had a rope steering system that didn't work too well. I also loved racing other kids across the pond on ice skates and seeing who could make it first to the store on their bicycle.

*Downhill Racing Cart (1926)*

107

# Never Say Die

Even the youngest sportsman is encouraged. Six year-old Cassandra is in a baseball clinic that meets twice a week. A group of parents volunteer to be coaches. The parents pitch to the kids, and hit high flies and grounders for the kids to field. There's an esprit de corps out there on the field, a feeling of closeness among parents and kids who are working together.

Playing together creates bonds among the players and strong friendships. People play sports for health and exercise, to compete against themselves or to compete against others, or just to have fun and to enjoy the companionship of other players. There are a wide range of sports played across America, and diverse ways in which people approach these sports. A player's experiences as an athlete, personal achievements, and moments in the limelight stay with one always, carrying over into other phases of life.

*Football Hero (1961)*

*Man Leaving Work to Go Golfing* (1919)

# Chapter 5
# Relaxation and Solitude

## Relaxing Times

Team sports appear to be for the young. Many people never have the opportunity or the inclination to participate in organized team sports.

Individual sports, such as running, hiking, sailing, skiing, and fishing, are ones that anybody can do at any age. These sports are used as a means of relaxation to many, a way to throw off the tensions of daily life. The participant in these is Everyperson. Everyperson is one who is in a Sunday morning tennis game or slips away for nine holes of golf after work. They stop at the downtown athletic club at lunchtime or after work to swim laps, play racquetball, or use the exercise equipment. Everyperson runs a couple of miles early each morning before work or late in the afternoon after work.

These sports are relaxing because they can be scheduled whenever it is convenient, and can be performed at whatever level is comfortable to the participant. They provide a release to physical and emotional tensions, and a feeling of healthy well-being.

# Mom's Time

Mom says, "It's great to get out, away from the children and household chores, and run. I look forward to the time alone, and I find that if I skip a couple of days, my muscles start screaming for me to get out there and run again."

"I enjoy jogging early in the morning, when the air seems relatively pure and free of automobile exhaust. I find jogging to be therapeutic; my tensions and bad thoughts simply dissolve. I find that because of jogging, I can better handle stressful situations at home and at the office."

"I find competition to be stressful. So what I like about running is that I can set my own goals, and don't have to measure up to anybody else. I can decide my own route and how fast I want to run. I can fit it into my day, whenever I have the time. I feel in charge and independent."

"Running gives me time to myself. I love my family, but I need to escape sometimes, to set aside a half-hour to clear my mind and have some solitude."

# The Lure of Sports

Individual sports can foster a feeling of responsibility and independence, of being master of your own fate.

Many enjoy sailing because, on the boat, they have the independence to make their own decisions. Adjusting the sails and choosing the sailing waters, give a feeling of great freedom.

*Waves of the Moon (1913)*

Often, the appeal of a sport is its closeness to nature and its distance from fellow human beings.

# Skiing

Skiing is an interesting sport because you can be surrounded by other people but still feel alone. You can meet people at the bottom of the hill and chat with them on the way up, but once at the top you're on your own to ski down alone and at your own speed.

If you are skiing on a long trail, you can find yourself all alone. You can go any speed you want and stop anywhere to enjoy the view from the mountains. Going down a slope, you are with others, but not talking and still somehow alone, feeling at one with the mountain, up high above the problems of mortals. It's exciting to get to the bottom, but also a shame; you've been brought back down to earth, back with the teeming humanity.

*The Winner Belongs to a Fisk Bicycle Club (1918)*

# Bicycling

Bicycling is a sport that can be social or for the loner. When a group meets for a biking outing, the route is planned for the day and arrangements are made to meet at nightfall. Then the group gets on the way.

Sometimes riding in small groups, but just as often, after settling in at an individual speed, one can bike alone. Back roads twist through small towns and mountain scenery. Occasionally, some of the riders meet, and stop to cool off in a stream or to buy an ice-cream sundae.

Sometimes circumstances cause other people to become involved. A bike overturned and the rider was taken into a nearby house to have a scraped knee attended to. Freshly baked apple pie and hot chocolate were handed round before everyone continued.

Bicycling for the large part of every day made the bike seemed to fit as comfortably as well-worn favorite clothes. The scenery passed by at first hand, now that one was no longer encased in a metal car and whizzing past. The pace was leisurely, and unexpected waterfalls, meandering streams, and even a small black bear pass by. The group rides in pouring rain, ponchos flying, feeling as though they are the only ones on the road. Bicycling makes people feel at one with nature.

# Hiking

Hiking in the mountains heightens the senses and both physical and emotional strength is gained from the experience. Back home, the memories of the fields of ferns shaded by the trees, and the blooms on the rhododendrons and mountain laurel are a source of pleasure. Hiking is an ideal way to get exercise, escape from daily life, and commune with nature. Hiking makes one feel physically tired and as though something worthwhile has been accomplished. Returning home, everyone feels refreshed and rejuvenated.

The family went hiking one day, to try out the experience before planning a hiking holiday. They were on a large trail when the youngest became tired and needed to sit down. As they sat, they watched other people walk by. There were babies in backpacks, couples with dogs, and cyclists. When hiking, people are so much friendlier and always say hello to each other. They know that everyone they meet on the trail has the same feeling of reverence about nature. Everyone is there for the same purpose, to enjoy and commune with nature.

The family walked up a trail to a place that had a mountain stream on one side and large rocks on the other side. They climbed the rocks and could see the birds in the bushes and the trail that went on and on. All felt pulled by the trail as it tunneled through the woods, wanting and needing to know where it led.

*Vacation: Boy Riding Goose (1934)*   117

# The Adventure of Sports

Sports can mean adventures as well as exercise. Skiing or hiking on a new trail is like starting out on a quest. You have a goal—to reach the bottom or top of the mountain—but you don't know what you will encounter along the way.

Uncle Jim described a hiking trip one day. "On a hiking trip, we took a five-mile hiking trail from one town to another several miles away. The trail took us up on the cliffs, high above the sea. The bushes were all overgrown, giving the trail an untraveled look. At one point, the path veered inland, through a turnstile into a large field. A sign said "Beware of the bull." We made it safely through the field, and then the trail turned back to parallel the sea. We were still feeling far from civilization when the path took a sharp curve. There, nestled below, the next town suddenly appeared, seemingly out of nowhere.

"In the lake district, we rented a canoe for a couple of days. We started out in a river, so narrow in places that we could reach out on either side and touch the bushes. Suddenly, we came out of our narrow waterway into a huge, sparkling lake. It was overwhelming to be, without notice, in the large expanse of the lake after the claustrophobic feeling of being hemmed in by trees and bushes."

In individual sports, as in team sports, some people push themselves to meet personal goals. They strive to run a greater distance or climb a higher mountain. Others enjoy the sport for the experience, for the pleasure of just doing it.

*The Mystery of the River Cave (1914)*

119

# Special Memories

Father and child fishing trips create special memories. The anticipation of waiting, then feeling the nibble and knowing a fish was there, are more important than catching the fish. Everyone knows about the big bass that got away. It isn't the fish that Dad or Sonny or Sister wants. It's just the process of catching it and the experience of being in the middle of the lake, where everything is quiet. The waves lap against the boat, the boat rocks, and the day lazes away.

*Fishing Grandfather and Boy (1954)*

# A Way of Life

Sports have a major influence on the lives of most Americans. As children, we get great pleasure playing games with our friends and families. Our daydreams are filled with sports fantasies, perhaps of stunning successes in the Olympics, or as professional athletes.

As we get older, sports become incorporated into our lives in many ways. We still enjoy playing, to keep ourselves fit, to relax, and to escape from the increased stresses of our lives. We get pleasure out of cheering for our local teams, still avid followers of the sports of our childhood dreams. We watch our own children, as they grow to become involved in their own sports, in their own way.

We are nostalgic about sports, remembering wistfully our heroes, our own unrepeatable successes on the playing field. We are surprisingly bound to each other by sports, as our interest and participation in sports unites us with family members, friends, and strangers.

*Hi-Yi-Deels (1916)*

# Picture Credits: